I have broken free

Ending the cycle of emotional neediness

Aimée Huard

Copyright © **Aimée Huard**, 2025

Table of Contents

Forward

Was there ever a time you were impatiently awaiting a text message from a loved one? That sinking feeling in your chest, the racing thoughts—*Did I say something wrong? Are they pulling away?* —and the overwhelming need to feel reassured that everything is okay? If you've ever been caught in this cycle of emotional turmoil, know that you are not alone. I've been there too. So many of us have.

Having experienced this reality myself, I wrote this book because I understand how suffocating emotional dependency can be. It takes over your life. Your sense of self is distorted, and you start to believe that other people are necessary for your happiness, value, and basic survival. I've discovered through my own experience, nevertheless, that you *can* escape.

This book covers more ground than simply getting over a toxic relationship or surviving a breakup. Going deeper is key to comprehending the causes of our initial emotional dependence. It's about owning up to the unhealed wounds we bear from our early years, prior traumas, or even social pressures that make us feel incomplete unless we have another person's love.

Regaining your power is the main theme of this book. It's about developing emotional independence—not in a way that constructs barriers around your heart, but rather in a way that enables you to love passionately while maintaining your integrity. The goal is to terminate the cycle of neediness, dread, and insecurity and create a life in which your enjoyment is independent of approval from others.

Turning through these pages will provide you with useful tips, thought-provoking activities, and practical tools that you can put to use right now. This is a road map for your recovery, development, and eventual success—it's not just theory. This book is designed to help you achieve the emotional independence you deserve, regardless of whether you're still coping with the fallout from a traumatic breakup or you've simply realised that emotional neediness has been preventing you from growing.

Breaking Free is a difficult process that takes time to achieve. However, you can come out stronger, more self-assured, and more in charge of your life if you have the patience, self-compassion, and courage to face your feelings.

Relationships based on love, respect, and trust rather than fear or dependence might be healthier.

Breathe deeply, then. You are on an adventure, and it starts right now. It is a privilege to walk with you as you discover your inner peace, embrace your true self, and become the self-assured, self-reliant person you were always destined to be.

Let's take this step together.

Introduction

Emotional reliance causes a unique type of pain—the kind that slowly gnaws at your self-esteem, erodes your peace of mind, and leaves you feeling as if your happiness is always at the whim of someone else. You'll know when you feel it. It's the moment you realise how much your life revolves around the attention, affection, and validation of another person. When they're present, you feel complete. But when they pull away, even little, it's as if the floor collapses beneath you, leaving you searching for security.

I've lived that reality and understand how weighty it may feel. I once believed that without my partner's affection and approval, I was nothing. When texts went unanswered, my imagination spiralled into feelings of rejection. My mood became wholly dependent on the behaviour of others—whether they were in a good mood, showed me love, or paid attention. Constant anxiety was draining.

Heartbreak for those of us who are emotionally reliant does not simply feel like the end of a relationship. It feels like we're losing ourselves. The overpowering sense of emptiness and terror stems not just from their absence, but also from our inability to recognise ourselves without them. In those instances, the agony is more than just losing someone. It's about losing the identity we created for them.

But what if I told you that this agony, while very real, is also your route to liberation?

Breaking the Cycle (Expectations on Your Journey)

Breaking away from emotional reliance does not imply "getting over" someone or simply moving on from sadness. It's about regaining oneself. It's about realising that your worth and happiness should never be dependent on someone else's presence in your life. It is about learning to stand on your own, to love without clinging, and to accept that you may be whole and happy without relying on others to fill in the gaps.

The process will not be easy. It is not a straightforward "one size fits all" trip. You'll have to tackle the deep-rooted concerns that have guided your relationships, as well as the unhealed scars you may not have even realised existed. There will be times when you feel lost, but that is part of the journey. You'll have to learn to tolerate discomfort rather than rush to fill the vacuum with someone else's love.

But let me assure you that you *can* break the cycle. You will *heal*. The fear of being alone, the need for constant reassurance, and the anxiety that dominates your thoughts will no longer hold as much control over you by the end of this journey. You will learn to love profoundly while remaining true to yourself. You will gain emotional independence, which will allow you to experience a level of calm and self-love that you may not be aware is attainable right now.

As you read this book, you'll come across practical tips that you may use right away. This book is your roadmap to daily healing and growth, with practical activities to help you recognise and overcome emotional triggers and introspective techniques to foster self-awareness. Every chapter will help you gain a better understanding of yourself and break free from the negative patterns that have held you captive for so long.

How to Use This Book for Daily Healing and Growth

I didn't want to write a book full of abstract principles that are difficult to put into action. My objective is to provide you with practical skills that you can use every day, no matter where you are on your journey. This book is intended to be interactive, with each chapter building on the previous one, allowing you to really reflect on your emotions, relationships, and life patterns that need to change. I recommend you to read this book slowly, one step at a time, and allow yourself to thoroughly absorb each section.

Each chapter concludes with exercises and journaling prompts designed to be incorporated into your daily life. These are more than just activities for self-reflection; they are tools for genuine change. Whether you're going through a breakup, dealing with persistent emotional dependency in your present relationship, or simply trying to improve your relationship with yourself, these activities will assist lead your healing journey. Use this book as a personal friend, something to refer to when you need advice or a reminder of your own power.

As you progress through the chapters, keep in mind that healing is not a linear process. There will be setbacks, and that is okay. Some days will be easier than others, and certain emotions may surface unexpectedly. Allow yourself grace during this process. Healing does not happen quickly, but with effort, introspection, and the practical tools outlined in this book, you *will* become stronger.

This book will guide you on a path to escape the cycle of emotional neediness and recover control of your happiness. You are not here to discover how to change other people, or to "fix" relationships that make you feel unworthy. You're here to heal *yourself*—to recapture your confidence, find serenity in solitude, and become the emotionally independent person you've always wanted to be.

Part I:

Recognizing and Understanding Emotional Dependency

1. Emotional Dependency

Emotional reliance is a deceptive thing. It initially feels like love. It feels like connection, passion, and a wonderful want to be close to someone. However, with time, that deep feeling of connection begins to devour you, taking over your thoughts and feelings. What begins as adoration quickly transforms into anxiety—an ongoing concern about whether you're enough, whether the relationship will endure, or whether your spouse actually loves you. When you're emotionally reliant, things don't always look or feel how we expect. It's not merely evident clinginess or a desire to be with someone all the time. Emotional dependency can manifest itself in subtle ways, seeping into daily routines, colouring your thoughts, and driving your emotions without your awareness.

Daily Signs You're Emotionally Dependent Without Realizing It

Maybe you thought, "I'm just a caring partner." I just want to know if they're okay. Or maybe you're constantly thinking about how someone else feels, losing sleep if they appear distant or distracted. Emotional dependency frequently manifests itself in tiny, everyday behaviours that might not appear problematic—until they begin to dictate your emotional landscape.

Sign #1: Your Happiness Depends on Their Mood.

One of the most obvious indicators of emotional reliance is when your daily happiness is influenced by your partner's mood. If they are pleasant, so are you. If they are distant or upset, you will sense it too. A partner's emotional state can affect anyone, but when it entirely controls your mood or sense of well-being, it may indicate dependency. This sets up a habit of "emotional mirroring," in which you feel responsible for improving their mood or see their terrible day as a reflection of your own incompetence.

Reflecting on the past, I recall feeling concerned if my partner appeared silent or distracted. Even if he was just weary from work, I would find myself agonising over what I had done wrong, repeating our previous conversations in my head, and altering my own attitude to match his. It wasn't until long later that I realised how much I relied on him for inner calm and pleasure.

Sign #2: You are constantly seeking reassurance.

Another common symptom is an ongoing need for reassurance. Do you constantly ask your partner if they still love you or if they are content in the relationship? Perhaps it's subtle, like fishing for praises or looking for signs that they're dedicated. This reliance on reassurance reveals a deep-seated insecurity that seeks affirmation from beyond rather than inside.

In my prior relationship, I was always asking my boyfriend how he felt about us. At first, it felt normal to desire to know. However, as time passed, I realised that his reassurance felt fleeting—I needed to hear it virtually every day to feel comfortable. This need for reinforcement grew stressful for both of us, and it eventually hindered me from developing confidence in myself.

Sign #3: Fear of Being Alone.

Many persons who struggle with emotional reliance experience anxiety or feelings of incompleteness when alone. They may struggle to fill their time without their spouse, and they may even avoid being alone by remaining in unsatisfactory relationships. This fear of being alone is typically an indication that you've come to regard your spouse as an emotional lifeline, someone who provides a sense of security that you don't yet know how to build for yourself.

Looking back, I recall feeling scared whenever my boyfriend proposed going on a weekend trip without me or spending time with friends. I was uncomfortable being alone with my thoughts, and the silence seemed oppressive. I used to think this was a statement of how much I loved him, but it was actually a reflection of my inability to be at ease with myself.

Sign #4: You are always adjusting to meet their needs.
An emotionally dependent individual will go out of their way to accommodate their partner's every need, even if it means sacrificing their own values, comfort, or happiness. You may find yourself saying "yes" to things you do not want to do or concealing aspects of yourself that you believe would not be favourably appreciated. You lose touch with who you truly are as a result of your constant focus on becoming what others want.

This habit of pleasing others in relationships has become second nature to me. I would go along with plans I didn't like, appear to like activities I wasn't interested in, and alter aspects of my personality to please my partner. I gradually lost sight of my own individuality, becoming a version of myself designed to please others rather than being genuine to myself.

Sign #5. You Struggled to Keep Your Own Identity

In emotionally dependent relationships, it is common to lose sight of who you are outside of the connection. Did you stop doing activities you used to enjoy, or did your social life revolve solely around your partner's schedule? Did you begin to identify yourself based on your function in the relationship rather than as a person with your own dreams, interests, and goals?

When emotional reliance takes hold, it may feel as if your identity is inextricably linked to being someone's partner. Before you're ever seen as "you," you're "so-and-so's girlfriend" or "so-and-so's wife". One of the most disempowering features of emotional dependence is a loss of self. You may have felt as if you no longer knew who you were or that your life was solely focused on the relationship.

In a good relationship, both parties retain their individuality while encouraging one other's personal progress. Emotional reliance, on the other hand, causes boundary blurring and a loss of identity.

Where Do You Stand on the Emotional Dependency Quiz?

Below is a quick questionnaire to help you figure out where you stand in terms of emotional reliance. This quiz is a simple tool to help you reflect on your relationship behaviours and attitudes. Take your time and be honest with yourself—this is a judgment-free zone for developing self-awareness.

1. How frequently do you experience anxiety or insecurity when your partner is inaccessible or distant?
- A) Almost never—I can remain confident in myself.
- B) It happens from time to time, but I typically recover.
- C) Frequently—I find myself worrying about them all the time.
- D) Always—I feel uneasy if I'm not linked to them.

2. Do you frequently seek reassurance from your partner about their feelings or the relationship?
- A) No, I'm confident in our relationship.
- B) Occasional, but only during difficult times.
- C) Frequently—I require constant reassurance to feel secure.
- D) Almost every day—I don't feel right without it.

3. How do you feel about spending time alone, without your partner?

- A) I appreciate my alone time; it is refreshing.
- B) I'm comfy, but I'd rather be with them.
- C) I feel anxious and dislike being alone.
- D) I avoid being alone because I feel lost without them.

4. Do you frequently sacrifice your own needs or preferences to keep your partner happy?
- A) No, I can voice my needs confidently.
- B) Occasionally, but I understand when to set boundaries.
- C) Frequently—I often agree to things in order to avoid disagreement.
- D) Always—I am worried I will lose them if I do not adapt.

5. How does your partner's negative mood influence you?
- A) I empathise, but it does not affect my mood.
- B) I am mildly impacted, but I am able to separate my emotions.
- C) I'm deeply moved and feel responsible for cheering them up.
- D) It completely alters my mood, and I remain nervous till they are fine.

Quiz Results: - Mostly A's: You demonstrate a strong sense of self and emotional independence. While you like your partner, you understand how to prioritise your own wants and feelings.

- Mostly B's: You demonstrate healthy independence but may still have moments of emotional dependency. This is natural, however you might want to focus on your self-confidence to feel more grounded.

- Mostly C's: You most likely look to your mate for security and happiness. Working on internal confidence and resilience may be effective.

- Mainly Ds: Emotional reliance has a huge impact on your well-being.

2. The Roots of Emotional Neediness

Emotional neediness does not appear out of nowhere; it frequently has deep roots in our history, shaped by the relationships, experiences, and traumas we carry from infancy and beyond. To completely break free from emotional dependency, we must go beneath the surface, investigate how our history moulds our desire for reassurance, approval, and connection.

Unhealed Wounds

Many of our emotional behaviours are influenced by what psychologists refer to as *attachment styles*, which develop during our early years. If you grew up with emotionally unavailable, critical, or inconsistent carers, you may have formed a *anxious attachment style*, which is characterised by feelings of insecurity in relationships and a reliance on others' reassurance.

For example, if a parent was warm and loving one moment then aloof or critical the next, you may have developed a desire for their approval but unsure when or if it will occur. This discrepancy causes internal unease and can leave you constantly seeking confirmation in your relationships. You may find yourself attempting to "earn" love, believing that if you are "good enough" or do everything "right," you will obtain the affection and stability you seek.

I recall conversing with a friend who described how her mother's critical behaviour made her feel inadequate from a young age. When her mother expressed affection, she felt worthy and lovable. However, the warmth was uneven, frequently replaced by criticism that made her feel like she'd never be good enough. As an adult, she frequently found herself in situations where she felt compelled to work endlessly for her partner's attention and acceptance. It wasn't until she realised that this pattern was caused by her relationship with her mother that she was able to start healing and breaking free from the cycle of emotional neediness.

Furthermore, past trauma can exacerbate these concerns. Perhaps you were abandoned, neglected, or had a horrible split in your prior relationship. These terrible events might heighten your dread of losing individuals you care about, resulting in an emotional dependency cycle. When you've been injured previously, it's natural to want to avoid being hurt again—but in doing so, we often end up repeating old habits and being locked in cycles of neediness.

Reflecting on Your Past

Understanding the causes of emotional reliance necessitates introspection. Our brains are programmed to follow patterns, and the patterns we encounter in our relationships frequently mimic those we seen or learnt as children. If you were continually vying for approval or learnt that love was conditional, you are likely to repeat this dynamic in your adult relationships unless you actively try to change it.

Take a minute to reflect on former relationships. Do you observe any recurring themes, such as a desire for validation, a fear of abandonment, or a preference for emotionally unavailable partners? These tendencies are not coincidental; they are frequently entrenched in our earliest relationships and experiences, when we first learnt what love, attention, and approval looked like.

One of the people I worked with said that she had frequently fallen for partners who were distant or unavailable. She realised, on consideration, that she was subconsciously duplicating her connection with her father, who was frequently physically present but emotionally absent. She was in relationships for years where she felt unworthy and had to chase her partner's affection and attention. When she recognised this pattern, she realised that her dependency was not about a specific relationship, but rather a cycle she had internalised since infancy. She then resolved to work over her fears, eventually changing her approach to relationships completely.

Recognising these patterns will help you recognise that emotional reliance is a learnt response, not an inherent problem. These cycles continue because they are familiar, and the mind seeks comfort in what it knows, even if it is painful. However, if you recognise these patterns for what they are, you may begin the road of changing them.

Exercises to Determine Your Emotional Triggers

Identifying emotional triggers is critical for recovery. Triggers are reactions caused by unresolved emotions or prior experiences, and they can help you understand why some situations elicit feelings of insecurity or neediness. The exercises below are intended to help you recognise these triggers and begin to understand the underlying beliefs or anxieties that cause them.

Exercise 1: The Trigger Journal

Take a moment to journal about any feelings of anxiety, neediness, or insecurity in your relationship. Write down the incident, your initial reaction, and any bodily symptoms you had (such as a racing heart or a tight chest). Then, ask yourself this:

1. What was I scared of in this moment?
2. What previous experience does this remind you of?
3. What do I think of myself in this situation?

Look deeper to see whether this feeling reminds you of anything from the past, such as being overlooked as a child or being rejected in a previous relationship. The belief could be, "I am only valuable if others pay attention to me." Understanding these fundamental assumptions is the first step towards questioning and changing them.

Exercise 2: Reframing your inner dialogue

Emotional neediness is frequently expressed through self-critical thoughts. If you find yourself thinking "I'm too needy," or "I'm afraid they'll leave me because I'm too much," it's time to question your self-talk. Instead of accepting these ideas as true, try reframing them.

Write down any critical ideas you have throughout the day, and then rework them in a more compassionate manner. For example,

- Original thought: "If they don't text me back, it means I'm not important to them."

- Reframed Thought: "Their delayed answer does not reflect my merit. My worth is independent of how frequently people contact me."

By frequently reframing your inner dialogue, you begin to alter the narrative you tell yourself about your value, progressively undermining your need for external validation.

Exercise 3: Mapping your Relationship Patterns
Consider your past relationships and seek for trends. Consider questions like:

- What attributes do I look for in partners?

- How do I usually react when I feel uncertain or insecure in a relationship?

- Do I notice myself repeating the same patterns, even with other partners?

Take notes on your reflections and see if any themes arise. If you find yourself drawn to unavailable companions or are constantly concerned about being abandoned, this may indicate unresolved ideas about love and relationships. Recognising these tendencies is essential to breaking away from them.

Exercise 4: Identifying Your "Inner Child" Wounds.
Unmet childhood needs are often the source of emotional dependency. Reflect on your earliest experiences of desiring attention, affirmation, or affection, and consider questions such as:
- Did I feel recognised and valued as I was?
- Was love freely given, or did I believe I have to earn it?
- Were my emotional needs met consistently, or were they frequently ignored?
Consider these recollections and allow yourself to experience any feelings that come up. Consider giving your younger self the love, acceptance, and validation that they required but may not have received. This activity is a gentle technique to identify and heal the scars that contribute to dependency.

Recognising your triggers, rethinking your beliefs, and understanding your habits can help you heal from the emotional traumas that drive dependency. This is not a quick or easy process, but each realisation brings you one step closer to breaking free from the cycle of neediness and learning to love yourself deeper. Healing these deep-rooted patterns is a journey, but it will lead you to the serenity, security, and independence you deserve.

3. Why We Struggle to Let Go After a Breakup

Breakups can be extremely painful, leaving us with doubts, insecurities, and fears. This conflict is driven by a deep desire for connection and the comfort of the familiar. Even if you knew the breakup was for the best, the hole left behind can be crushing. In this chapter, we'll look at why breakups may be so painful, examine the hidden power dynamics in emotional relationships, and discover how to cope with the loss without losing yourself.

Why Breakups Strike So Hard

One of the most prevalent concerns people have following a breakup is the fear of being alone. It is normal to seek connection and companionship, but when our self-worth is linked to being in a relationship, being alone can feel like an existential crisis. For other people, the dread of loneliness is so intense that it keeps them imprisoned in bad relationships, scared of the empty space on the other side.

I recall conversing with a friend who admitted that she stayed in a bad relationship for years because she dreaded the notion of being alone. Her relationship had become her identity, and quitting it felt like giving up a piece of herself. This anxiety, she realised, was about more than just losing her boyfriend; it was about losing the life and stability she had grown to identify with him. "Who am I without this relationship?" she would ask herself, as if the presence of another person had obscured her own identity.

This dread is frequently based on our self-image. For many people, loneliness is a reflection of their worth, as if being alone proves that they aren't worthwhile or lovable enough to be selected by someone else. People frequently feel this way, yet it is a misconception. Breakups do not determine your worth, nor do they mean you will be alone forever. Recognising that the dread of being alone has nothing to do with your fundamental worth is the first step towards learning to cope.

Recognising the Power Imbalance in Your Emotional Attachments

Emotional reliance in many relationships results in an underlying power imbalance. One spouse may become the source of affirmation, security, and joy for the other. Over time, this relationship can create an imbalance in which one person has emotional "power" over the other. When a relationship ends, the more dependent person typically feels as if they have lost something much bigger than a partner—they believe they have lost the source of their pleasure, safety, and self-worth.

A former client once stated how she became so emotionally attached to her partner that she saw him as the "solution" to all of her difficulties. She was upset when he stopped the relationship, not just because of the loss, but also because she felt like she didn't have someone to "complete" her. She had unknowingly given him her emotional power. After the relationship ended, she felt helpless and powerless because of this imbalance.

Recognising and addressing this power imbalance is critical to healing. It is natural to feel strongly attached to someone we care about, but when that connection turns into reliance, we give up control over our pleasure. By recovering that power, you can begin to understand that your well-being is something you can grow and maintain on your own, rather than relying on others. Understanding this helps to demolish the myth that losing a relationship entails losing oneself.

Coping With Breakup Without Losing Yourself

Learning to let go after a breakup is a process that takes self-compassion, patience, and practical actions for regaining emotional independence. Here are some methods for dealing with loss without losing yourself in the process.

1. Reconnect with Yourself and Reclaim Your Identity

After putting so much effort into a relationship, it's easy to lose sight of who you are on your own. Now is the moment to reconnect with yourself by pursuing your hobbies, passions, and dreams outside of the relationship. Ask yourself the following questions:

- Before I met my partner, what did I enjoy?
- What activities make me feel energised and fulfilled?
- How do I want to advance both personally and professionally in the future?

Rediscovering oneself may be a tremendously satisfying process. One acquaintance who had went through a breakup decided to go on a solo road trip, which she had always wanted to do but never did because her spouse wasn't interested. On that trip, she reconnected with her boldness, independence, and spirit of adventure. She returned with a stronger sense of self and greater resilience, realising that she didn't need someone else to complete her; she was entire on her own.

2. Develop a Self-Care Routine to Support Your Emotional Health

A breakup can leave you feeling vulnerable, so developing a self-care routine can be really reassuring. Simple techniques like as writing, meditation, and spending time with supportive people can all provide emotional support and help you process your emotions. Journaling, in particular, may be a great technique for releasing repressed emotions and gaining understanding about your experiences.

One woman mentioned that after her separation, she spent fifteen minutes each morning journaling about her emotions. She would express her anguish, irritation, and perplexity without condemnation. She discovered that writing about her emotions helped her relieve her suffering and see things more objectively over time. It became a daily self-validation practice for her, helping her to process emotions she might have otherwise suppressed.

3. Establish Boundaries and Limit Contact

If possible, limit communication with your ex, especially in the early phases. Maintaining continual communication or often checking their social media profiles can be detrimental to the healing process. It's natural to be inquisitive about what they're up to, yet each interaction reopens old hurts and leaves you trapped in the past. Setting limits, such as deleting their phone number or taking a break from social media, can assist you in creating the emotional space required for healing.

One man I know blocked his ex on social media after finding himself going through her posts late at night, which left him feeling sad and uneasy. Although it was difficult, he realised that separating himself was an act of self-care, allowing him to concentrate on his own recovery rather than remaining emotionally involved with someone who was no longer in his life.

4. Swap Negative Self-Talk for Positive Affirmations
Following a breakup, it is natural to have self-doubt and negative thoughts such as "I wasn't good enough" or "I'll never find love again." These beliefs can trap you in misery and uncertainty. Replace negative thoughts with affirmations that help you focus on your value and strengths, reminding yourself that you are lovable, valuable, and capable of healing.

Write affirmations like:

- I am whole and complete in my current state.
- I deserve love, peace, and happiness.
- My enjoyment is ingrained within me.

Daily repetition of these affirmations can gradually replace negative thinking with a more powerful perspective, allowing you to recover your self-esteem.

5. Seek Help From Trusted Friends or a Therapist

Breakups can be isolating, but you don't have to go through it alone. For support, seek help from friends, family, or a therapist. Talking openly with people can provide relief and new insights, allowing you to see things in a new way. Professional assistance may be required at times to address deeper concerns and unhealed wounds.

One lady stated that treatment became a lifeline for her following her breakup. During her sessions, she realised that her relationship to her ex stemmed from a childhood need for approval. Therapy assisted her in addressing her inner traumas, ultimately leading to a sense of calm and independence she had never experienced before.

Final Thoughts on letting Go

The end of a relationship may feel like the end of the world, but it is also a new beginning. Learning to let go without losing yourself is about rediscovering your inner strength and recognising that you are entire, whether or not you are in a relationship. Each action you take to regain your sense of self, develop your confidence, and care for your emotional well-being will get you closer to achieving independence and serenity.

Part II:

Step-by-Step Guidance to Heal After a Breakup

4. Allowing Yourself to Grieve

The breakdown of a relationship might set off a grieving process similar to that of any other significant loss. It's tempting to attempt to get over this discomfort quickly, to divert yourself, or to completely avoid it. However, allowing yourself to completely experience the sadness associated with a breakup is critical for long-term healing and progress.

Why You Need to Feel Pain to Heal Pain

Grief, as unpleasant as it is, is a normal component of the recovery process. Avoiding or repressing emotions may seem like the simplest solution in the short term, but it frequently results in enduring unhappiness, bitterness, and unresolved issues. When you avoid grieving, you bring unresolved emotional baggage into future relationships, making it difficult to establish true bonds. Healing from a breakup isn't about rapidly getting over someone; it's about thoroughly experiencing the loss before letting it go.

One friend told me how, after a devastating breakup, she pushed herself into work, keeping herself busy to avoid feeling the weight of her despair. She persuaded herself she was "doing fine" since she wasn't crying, but her feelings were festering on the inside. It wasn't until she allowed herself to face her sadness—crying, contemplating, and mourning the relationship—that she felt lighter and more at ease. Allowing herself to feel the grief allowed her to heal and emancipated her from her emotional dependent on her ex.

Recognising your pain does not imply lingering on it indefinitely, but rather allowing yourself to experience what you feel without judgement. Allow yourself to be sad, and remember that it is normal to lament the loss of something valuable. Accepting this process is a sign of self-compassion and a significant step towards true healing.

A Daily Habit for Processing Grief

Journaling is one of the most effective strategies to go with grief. When you write, you create a safe environment in which to openly express your emotions, helping you to let go of what you've been holding inside without fear of being judged. Daily journaling can help you detect patterns in your thoughts, identify emotional triggers, and figure out where your pain is coming from. It can act as a mirror, reflecting the depths of your emotions and assisting you in achieving clarity during times of emotional turbulence.

Begin each journaling session by writing whatever comes to mind, without censorship. You may begin with prompts like:

- How am I feeling right now?
- What memories or thoughts are rising today?
- What am I frightened of during my recovery process?
- How has this connection affected my life? What did it teach me?

One lady who journaled on a regular basis following a breakup admitted that she was initially frustrated because writing about her emotions didn't immediately improve her mood. However, when she reflected on her entries, she noticed how her feelings were changing. She observed flashes of hope replacing her despair, and she could feel herself slowly letting go. Journaling became a ritual, a type of self-therapy that allowed her to express her emotions rather than suppress them.

Putting thoughts on paper allows you to externalise your emotions, making them easier to understand and regulate. As you write, you'll see that grief has a rhythm—it ebbs and flows—and that allowing it room honours your experience, which is necessary for actual healing.

How to Make Space for Genuine Healing

One of the most difficult things of moving on after a relationship is keeping your distance from your former. The "No-Contact Rule" is a common yet effective method for creating the distance needed to fully recover. This rule prohibits you from making any contact with your ex for a specified amount of time, including messaging, calling, or checking their social media. While this may appear excessive, the goal is to eliminate daily reminders of the connection and allow yourself to focus on your own recovery without hindrance.

The no-contact period allows you to rediscover yourself, reclaim your independence, and create an emotional distance from the relationship. One lady described how the first few weeks of no communication were absolutely unbearable—she found herself craving for updates, wanting to check in, and wondering if he was thinking about her. However, as time passed, she found that her feelings for her ex began to wane. Without the everyday reminders, she may begin to reinvent her identity outside of the partnership. She started investing in hobbies, socialising with friends, and focussing on her goals. By the end of the no-contact time, she felt a surge of strength and independence.

The No-Contact Rule also decreases the risk of reverting to previous behaviours or becoming involved in emotional back-and-forths, which can make it difficult to move ahead. During this time, you may still experience feelings of sadness, nostalgia, or even rage, but every time you resist the urge to reach out, you take a step closer to emotional independence. By setting this boundary, you reclaim control of your recovery path.

Tips for implementing no-contact:

- Set a Timeframe: Commit to a timeframe that works for you, such as 30, 60, or 90 days. Having a timetable might make the task seem more manageable.
- Block Social Media: Unfollow, mute, or temporarily block your ex from social media. Out of sight might genuinely be out of mind, giving you the opportunity to focus on yourself.
- Create a "Reaching Out" Journal: If you feel compelled to contact your ex, record your feelings in a notebook instead.

Pouring your feelings onto the page can help you get rid of the impulse without risking a physical interaction.

5. Dealing with Emotional Flashbacks

Moving on from a relationship entails more than just coping with loss and accepting that someone is no longer in your life. For many, the real struggle is dealing with emotional flashbacks—sudden, strong memories of your ex that come back when you least expect them. These memories can be triggered by anything: a familiar song, a perfume, a location you used to visit together, or even a fleeting idea.

How to Deal With Triggers That Bring Back Memories of Your Ex

When you're going through a breakup, your mind often clings to the memories you had with your ex—the inside jokes, the long discussions, the habits you formed together. These memories become mental markers, and even after the relationship ends, your brain retains them, reliving them as if they were still there. Emotional flashbacks might feel like a tidal surge of emotions, transporting you back to a period when your relationship was vibrant and healthy. It can feel like you're being pulled backward, away from the success you've fought so hard to achieve.

One woman described how the fragrance of fresh coffee in the morning would throw her into a tailspin, reminding her of languid Sunday mornings spent with her ex. She'd pass past a coffee shop, catch a whiff of the aroma, and be quickly transported back to her kitchen, laughing and enjoying priceless moments. She would go from feeling confident and strong to painfully missing him. Every time this happened, she became irritated with herself, as if she had taken two steps forward and three steps back.

If you are having comparable flashbacks, know that they do not reverse your progress. Emotional flashbacks are common and part of the healing process. The goal is to receive them without judgement. Instead of blaming yourself or assuming that these sentiments indicate that you are "not over" your ex, acknowledge that memories and emotions will linger while you heal. What you're experiencing is merely a memory resurfacing—one that you can accept and let go of, like a wave returning to the sea.

Here are some suggestions for dealing with these situations should they arise:
- Acknowledge the recollection: Tell yourself, "This is just a memory; it's okay to feel this way." Labelling it as a

recollection rather than present reality will help you stay grounded.

- Redirect your thoughts: Once you've acknowledged the flashback, gently return your attention to the present. Look around, take in your surroundings, and remind yourself that you're embarking on a new chapter in your life.

Create a "Healing Mantra": Choose a simple phrase to tell yourself in these moments, such as "I am healing," or "I am letting go, day by day." Repeating this mantra can help you relax and remind yourself of your progress.

Meditation and Grounding Techniques to Calm Your Mind

When emotional flashbacks are severe, practicing grounding techniques and meditation can be lifesaving. These practices ground you in the present moment, soothing your mind and allowing you to find equilibrium in the middle of a storm of memories. Grounding techniques reconnect you to the physical world, helping you to separate from emotional turmoil and return to a condition of calm. Meditation, on the other hand, enables you to watch your thoughts without passing judgement, allowing you to let go of lingering memories without becoming lost in them.

One man I met explained that everytime he thought about his ex, he felt a tightness in his chest, which was a physical expression of his emotional agony. He began employing grounding techniques whenever these emotions got overwhelming. He discovered that focussing on the present moment and reconnecting with his body—by touching something cold, observing the texture of a cloth, or feeling his feet firmly on the ground—helped him relieve stress. He regarded it as an "anchor" that saved him from becoming swept up in the waves of emotion.

Here are a few grounding techniques and meditation practices that can help you relax:

1. The 5-4-3-2-1 Technique

The 5-4-3-2-1 approach is a strong grounding practice that helps you refocus on the present moment by engaging your senses:

- 5: Look around and identify five items you observe.

- 4: List four items you can touch.

- 3: Identify three sounds you hear.

- 2: Pay attention to two items you can smell.

- 1: Name something you can taste.

By using your senses in this way, you are reconnecting with the physical world and reminding yourself that you are present, but your ex is not.

2. Focused Breath

When emotional flashbacks occur, they might generate anxiety, resulting in shallow and fast breathing. Deep, concentrated breathing can assist decrease your pulse rate and relieve tension in your body.

- Take a deep breath in through your nose and count to four.
- Hold your breath for four counts.
- Exhale slowly through your mouth for a count of four.
- Repeat this cycle several times, concentrating on the sensation of the breath travelling in and out of your body.

Focused breathing is easy yet extremely effective. When you actively slow your breathing, your mind follows suit, reducing the severity of the flashback and giving you a sense of serenity.

3. Visual Meditation: The "River of Thoughts" Exercise.

Visual meditation is an effective approach to control disturbing memories by allowing you to see your ideas as fleeting. Consider sitting on the bank of a peaceful river. Visualise your ex's thoughts and memories as leaves floating down a river. Allow each leaf to flow by without grabbing or holding it.

As you practise, try not to pass any judgement on the thoughts that arise. Simply watch the leaves—your memories and emotions—float down the river and out of sight. This visualisation serves as a reminder that all ideas, including painful ones, will pass.

4. Practice Self-Compassion

Emotional flashbacks might prompt self-criticism. You may find yourself thinking, "I should be over this by now," or, "Why can't I just move on?" Self-compassion involves treating yourself with love and empathy, especially when you are hurting. Remind yourself that healing is not a linear process, and that each memory is an opportunity to show yourself patience and love.

To cope with emotional flashbacks, one woman I know started practicing self-compassion meditation on a daily basis. She would close her eyes, place a palm over her heart, and tell herself, "I'm doing my best." "I deserve kindness and patience." Over time, this exercise helped her move past her flashbacks with acceptance rather than frustration, allowing her to recover from a place of calm rather than conflict.

Daily Affirmations to Stop Reliving the Past

The following are some daily affirmations that will assist you in letting go of the past and concentrating on the creation of a future that is calm and fulfilling:

1. "I release all thoughts of what could have been, and I welcome what is yet to come."

2. "I am worthy of peace and happiness, and I choose to cultivate it in my life each day."

3. "The past is a chapter that I have read,I am at liberty to compose a fresh narrative."

4. "I honor the lessons of my past without letting them control my present."

5. "I am growing stronger and wiser with each experience, and I move forward with grace."

6. "My heart is healing, and I am open to new possibilities."

7. "I am enough, just as I am, and I find joy within myself."

8. "Every day, I create space for joy, growth, and self-love."

9. "I forgive myself and others, releasing any weight that holds me back."

10. "I am free from the chains of the past; I embrace the beauty of now."

11. "I am resilient, and I trust myself to build a brighter future."

12. "I am thankful for the love I have experienced, and I am excited for the love I am creating for myself."

13. "I am focused on what lies ahead, grateful for all I have yet to experience."

14. "I trust the process of healing and know that each day brings me closer to peace."

15. "I am at home within myself, finding strength and joy in my own company."

Try choosing one or two affirmations each day, repeating them carefully, and letting each phrase resonate with you. Over time, these affirmations can help shift your emphasis from the past to the possibilities ahead, promoting a sense of self-love and inner calm.

6. Rebuilding   Self-Worth After a Breakup

One of the most difficult aspects of a breakup is the feeling of losing a part of yourself. Often, our self-worth is inextricably linked to the validation we receive from our spouse, leaving us feeling hollow and uncertain when the relationship ends. However, just because a relationship has ended does not imply that your value has decreased; rather, it means you now have the opportunity to find your worth in a new, meaningful way. Rebuilding self-esteem after a breakup is a process of self-discovery and empowerment. It's about discarding the layers of validation we've grown to expect from others and learning to accept ourselves completely, flaws and all. Every day, you take strides towards profound, long-term self-worth by recognising your intrinsic value, cultivating self-esteem via everyday routines, and freeing yourself from the judgements of others.

Recognising Your Value Outside of Relationships

Following a breakup, it is easy to question your worth. You can be left thinking, "Was I not good enough?" or "Did I do something wrong?" This way of thinking keeps you in a loop of self-blame, but keep in mind that your value is independent of your relationship status. You are intrinsically valued because of who you are, not because of others' presence in your life.

One lady told me that after their separation, she felt lost and unfinished. She had based so much of her identity on her relationship that when it ended, she felt as if she didn't know who she was without him. Through self-reflection, she gradually realised that her value had always existed—it had not vanished with the relationship. She began rediscovering satisfaction in her favourite activities, reconnecting with friends, and focussing on her own goals. She realised that the love and validation she had been looking for from her partner could be found within herself.

To begin recognising your value outside the relationship:
- **Consider Your Strengths and Qualities**: Make a list of the qualities that distinguish you from others. Are you empathetic? Creative? Resilient? Concentrate on what you contribute to the world, not just a relationship.
- **Revisit Your Passions and Interests**: Reconnect with any hobbies or goals you've set aside. Whether it's painting, volunteering, or learning a new skill, rediscovering what

makes you happy is an effective way to boost your self-esteem.

Remember Your Achievements: Consider what you've accomplished on your own—personal milestones, career successes, or instances when you demonstrated strength and resilience. These accomplishments demonstrate your worth regardless of any relationship.

Practical Exercises to Boost Self-Esteem Daily

Building self-esteem after a breakup takes time, but little, daily activities can have a significant impact on how you perceive yourself. Here are some practical exercises to help you improve your self-esteem every day:

1. **The "Mirror Talk" Exercise.**

This simple but effective technique consists of speaking positively to yourself in the mirror every morning. Begin by staring in your own eyes and listing three things you appreciate about yourself—qualities, skills, or even how you showed up today. For example: "I am compassionate," "I am strong and resilient," or "I have a kind heart." This exercise helps reinforce a good self-image, even on days when you may feel uncertain.

2. Daily Accomplishment Journal

Each evening, jot down three accomplishments you completed that day, no matter how tiny. It could be as simple as finishing a job project, going for a walk, or preparing a lovely supper. The idea is to recognize your efforts and instill confidence in your talents. Over time, this regular routine might let you recognise how capable you truly are.

3. Practicing Self-Compassion

Breakups might make you more critical of yourself, especially if you're dealing with feelings of regret or guilt. Self-compassion involves treating oneself with care and empathy. When you notice yourself thinking badly, try to reframe them. For instance, replace "I'm so stupid for trusting them" with: "I did my best in that relationship, and I'm learning from this experience."

4. Setting Small and Achievable Goals

Self-esteem grows when you have a sense of purpose and progress. Set one little objective per day, such as cleaning your bed, taking a short walk, or reading a few pages of a book. Completing minor goals boosts self-confidence and good momentum.

5. Affirmations of Self-Worth

Begin each day with affirmations that reinforce your self-worth. Simple words such as "I am whole and complete as I am," or "My worth is inherent and does not depend on anyone else" might help to establish a good tone for the day. Recite them aloud or write them down.

How to Avoid Defining Yourself Based on Others' Opinions

Many of us grow up believing that our worth is determined by other people's acceptance. However, identifying yourself based on the opinions of others causes unease, especially when those judgements are contradictory or critical. Reclaiming your feeling of self-worth entails prioritising your own viewpoint over all others.

One lady told a dramatic narrative of how, following her breakup, she was shattered by the judgements of friends and relatives who blamed her for the relationship's conclusion. She had an intense need to improve herself in order to regain their acceptance. However, through self-reflection and counselling, she realised that her happiness didn't have to be determined by what others thought of her decisions. She gradually began to organise her life around her own principles and views. She realised that the only opinion that really counted was her own.

Stop defining yourself based on others' opinions:
- **Set Boundaries for Feedback**: Not all feedback is worthy of your attention. Decide who's comments truly help you improve, and stay away from those that weaken your confidence.

- **Reframe Negative Feedback**: When someone criticises you, consider whether it is constructive or just their point of view. Understand how people frequently reflect their own insecurities onto others. Their opinions are about themselves, not you.

- **Defining Your Own Success**: Set personal goals based on your own ideals rather than those of society or others. Write down what success means to you, whether it's emotional independence, professional accomplishments, or simply feeling calm. When you follow your own idea of success, external opinions have less influence on you.

- **Strengthen Your Inner Voice:** Spend time each day listening to your own ideas and reflecting on what is actually important to you. Develop an inner voice that is uplifting and nonjudgmental. Remind yourself every day that you are enough just the way you are, without the need for approval from others.

- **Surround Yourself with Supportive individuals**: Spend time with individuals who value you for who you are, rather than what you can accomplish for them. Choose friends and mentors who will encourage you and appreciate your journey.

Part III:

Understanding and Managing Your Emotions

7. What Are Your Emotions Telling You?

Emotions, particularly after a breakup, can feel like an unending, overwhelming torrent that never stops, whether you're ready or not. Sadness, worry, fear, and even fury can feel like unwelcome guests, arriving unexpectedly and lasting far longer than we'd choose. However, within each of these feelings is a message waiting to be heard—a message that, if we learn to listen to, might lead us closer to knowing ourselves and, ultimately, healing.

I recall my own emotional path following a devastating breakup. The despair and worry seemed never-ending, and the anxiety felt like a weight on my chest that wouldn't let go. For a long time, I attempted to ignore it by busy myself with work, going out with friends, and doing whatever I could to drive these feelings away. But no matter what I did, the emotions would return when I was alone, telling me that I hadn't really listened to them yet.

This is not an easy trip, but it is incredibly rewarding. When you learn to listen to your emotions, they become guides on your journey to self-discovery and healing.

Listen to the Messages Behind Your Anxiety, Sadness, and Fear

When I finally stopped running from my emotions and started listening to them, I realised that each one had a valuable lesson. My nervousness indicated that I was terrified of being alone, that I feared the future without someone by my side. My melancholy reminded me of the love I had shared and lost, a love that still mattered even though it was no longer in my life. And my worry spoke to the uncertainty that lay ahead, an uncharted route that seemed terrible without the security of a familiar hand to clasp.

Anxiety: Anxiety usually emerges when we feel unsafe or uncertain. After a breakup, this sensation might become intensified as we face an unfamiliar and uncertain life. But instead of viewing anxiety as a threat, what if we saw it as a signal, a means for our bodies to warn us about our deeper worries and vulnerabilities? Anxiety is typically a symptom that you don't feel safe or supported. The anxiety of facing life alone, combined with the responsibility of reconstructing my identity, kept me uneasy.

Sadness: Sadness is frequently a response to loss, and it asks us not only to mourn the relationship we've lost, but also to honour the emotions, memories, and even dreams that accompanied it. Sadness is not something to "get over," but rather something to accept and experience. It reaffirms our capacity for love, connection, and vulnerability. For me, sitting with my pain highlighted how much I had invested in the relationship and helped me understand why it was so difficult to let go. It was my heart's way of honouring the love I previously felt, even though it was time to go on.

Fear: Fear of the unknown is powerful, especially when we are unexpectedly thrown into a future that differs from what we had envisioned. Fear frequently stems from a lack of control and the unknown possibilities that ahead. For me, fear was my mind's method of emphasising my unwillingness to change, my concern about embarking on a new chapter without a clear direction. Listening to that fear taught me that I needed to take things one day at a time, believing that I could construct a future even if it looked different from what I had envisioned.

When we take the time to pause and listen, our emotions disclose layers of our inner reality, allowing us to see past the surface sorrow and discover the teachings beneath. They identify our deepest needs and direct us towards healing. Rather than blaming ourselves for experiencing these things, we might begin to see our emotions as signals pointing us to what needs our attention the most.

Learning to sit with your emotions instead of running from them

Sitting with painful emotions is one of the most difficult things we can do. When confronted with the sting of loss or the rawness of anxiety, the desire to distract yourself or numb the emotion can be overwhelming. I understand this well because I spent months running away from my emotions following my split, occupying every moment with distractions. However, no matter how far I ran, the emotions would reappear the moment I was alone.

Finally, I decided to do something different: I would allow myself to feel. I recall sitting alone in my room one night, purposefully choosing to be with my feelings. The sadness came first, accompanied by a rush of tears that I had been holding back. Then came the fear—the uncertainty of beginning over, the question of whether I'd ever feel complete again. I was astonished by how intense these feelings were, but after allowing them to flow, I felt lighter. I realised I didn't need to fix the pain right away. All I needed to do was let it be, without judgement.

Here are several ways you might practise sitting with your emotions, allowing them to guide you rather than overwhelm you.

1. **Reserve Time for Feeling**: Find a quiet place where you may be alone without interruptions. Take a few deep breaths while comfortably seated or lying down. Allow whatever emotions occur to surface. Don't rush to analyse or "fix" things; simply feel.

2. **Label Your Emotions:** Naming how you're feeling can help you build distance. Say to yourself, "I'm feeling anxious," or "I'm feeling deeply sad right now." This simple process of labelling allows you to examine the emotion without becoming completely overwhelmed by it.

3. **Allow for Physical Sensations**: Emotions frequently appear physically. Anxiety may feel like a constriction in your chest, but melancholy may feel like heaviness in your shoulders. Try to observe these experiences without judgement. This phase helps you to feel the feeling as energy passing through you, rather than something to reject.

4. **Practise Deep Breathing:** When emotions are high, deep breathing can help you ground yourself. Inhale gently, hold for a time, then exhale deeply. This activates the parasympathetic nerve system, which can diminish the physical intensity of the feeling and make you feel more grounded.

5. **Journal Your Experience**: Writing down how you're feeling is an effective technique to handle emotions. After you've sat with your emotions, spend a few moments to record any insights or observations. Writing might help you make sense of what you're experiencing and recognise trends across time.

6. **Remind Yourself:** This, Too, Will Pass: Emotions are only transitory. When you feel as if your grief or anxiety will endure forever, remember that emotions come in waves. They climb, peak, and then sink. Holding onto this fact might give you the strength to face your emotions without fear of being overwhelmed.

By learning to sit with your feelings, you are developing a resilience that will serve you well after this split. When you allow yourself to feel entirely, you give yourself the opportunity to heal completely. Each emotion has something to teach you, and by embracing them rather than avoiding them, you give yourself the gift of genuine, authentic healing.

My Final Thoughts on What Your Emotions Tell You

Listening to your emotions is not about seeking immediate relief or solutions. It is about developing a sense of empathy and compassion for yourself. Each feeling, whether sad, fearful, or anxious, conveys a message, reminding you of your humanity, ability to love, and courage to heal.

If you allow yourself to sit with your emotions and listen to what they are saying you, you will come away from this experience with a better understanding of who you are. You'll learn that your emotions, rather than impeding you, are guiding you to self-discovery and inner serenity. Accept each feeling as a teacher, understanding that by allowing yourself to feel it, you are taking another step towards a more complete, stronger, and resilient self.

8. Ending the Cycle of Negative Thoughts

After a breakup, it's easy to become caught up in a negative spiral. Memories loop, regrets reappear, and you find yourself lost in terrible **"what-ifs."** These thoughts can be difficult to overcome, especially if you are feeling vulnerable. But here is the truth: *the thoughts you entertain have a huge impact on your reality.* When you learn to regulate and replace negative thinking with positive and hopeful perspectives, you make a significant step towards recovery. This chapter will walk you through the power of thought, practical strategies for interrupting negative thought patterns, and visualisation techniques to help you develop a more positive emotional state.

The Power of Thought: How Your Mind Affects Your Healing.

Thoughts are really powerful. They form our emotions, impact our choices, and, ultimately, how we perceive ourselves and the world. When we are caught up in negative thinking, it might feel as if there is no way out of the misery, as if every bad thought only adds to the fire. After my own breakup, my thoughts would spiral into "I'll never be good enough," "Maybe I deserved this," or "I'm not capable of being truly happy." These thoughts caused me to feel confined and helpless. But I realised that just because a concept crossed my head did not mean it was true or that I had to embrace it.

Consider this: if you continuously tell yourself that you are inadequate or unloveable, those thoughts will harden, sustaining a cycle of suffering and self-doubt. On the other side, by being aware of these patterns and replacing them with more constructive beliefs, you give yourself a significant gift: the opportunity to create a new reality based on personal growth and acceptance. This transition does not occur overnight, but even little actions can have a significant impact.

Practical Steps to Challenge and Replace Negative Thinking

Breaking the pattern of negative thinking needs mindfulness, patience, and effort. Here are some practical steps to help you recognise and replace negative thoughts with healthier, more powerful ones:

1. **Recognise Thought Patterns.** The first step is to recognise when you're stuck in a negative mental pattern. Typical patterns include:

- All-Or-Nothing Thinking: "If I'm not with them, I'll never be happy."
- Oversimplification: "Every relationship I have ends badly."
- Mind Reading: "They probably think I'm a failure."
- Catastrophising: "This breakup will ruin my life."

When a negative idea arises, pause and try to determine which of these patterns it belongs to. By doing so, you begin to recognise the concept for what it is: a distortion rather than the truth.

2. **Reframe Using Balanced Thinking:** When you recognise a negative thinking, ask yourself whether there is another, more balanced viewpoint. For example, if you're thinking, "I'll never be happy again," try reframing it as, "I'm going through a tough time right now, but happiness is possible for me in the future." Balanced thinking acknowledges your grief while also providing hope and possibility.

3. **Maintain A Thought Journal:** Writing down your negative ideas and challenging them in a notebook can be really beneficial. When you see yourself thinking negatively, note it down, recognise the thought pattern, and write a fresh, more positive perspective. Over time, you'll realise how frequently these thoughts arise—and how skilled you are at reframing them.

4. **Use "Evidence" to Counter the Thought:** If the idea "I'll never be loved" occurs, counter it by recalling moments when you were liked or respected by others. By focusing on evidence that contradicts the negative thought, you might reduce its effect on you. It is not about rejecting your emotions, but rather about gaining a more objective perspective.

5. **Practice self-compassion:** Self-criticism is frequently the root cause of negative thoughts. Self-compassion can help change your inner conversation from harsh to supportive. When you find yourself thinking badly, try responding like you would to a friend in the same situation: with empathy and encouragement. Remind yourself that it is normal to struggle and that healing is a process, not a race.

Visualisation Techniques for Developing Positive Emotions

Visualisation is an effective strategy for overcoming negative ideas and creating happy feelings. By using your imagination, you can build mental images of calm, joy, and resilience, which will assist to remodel your brain over time.

1. **The Safe Place Visualisation**: This is a simple technique in which you close your eyes and visualise a place where you are fully safe, comfortable, and content. It could be a real place from your history or an imagined destination. Spend a few minutes imagining the sights, sounds, and scents of this place. When you're feeling overwhelmed, return to this safe haven in your mind and allow it to ground you and bring you peace.

2. **Positive Visualisation of the Future:** Imagine yourself happy and content in six months or a year from now. Imagine what you're doing, who you're with, and how it feels. Visualise yourself enjoying the life you desire, free of the anguish of the breakup. This practice encourages hope and resilience by directing your attention on what is possible rather than what has been lost.

3. **The "Inner Light" Visualisation:** Sit quietly, close your eyes, and envision a soft, warm light shining in the centre of your chest. Imagine this light flowing throughout your body, infusing you with calm, self-love, and positivity. Allow this light to become brighter as you imagine it growing beyond you, engulfing the room, and eventually the entire space surrounding you. This visualisation serves as a reminder of your inner power and ability to heal on your own.

4. **Gratitude Visualisation:** Spend a few minutes every day visualising what you're grateful for. Consider moments of delight, individuals who care about you, or simple pleasures like a gorgeous sunrise or a warm cup of tea. Gratitude focusses your attention away from what you lack and towards what you have, improving your mood and lowering the power of negative thinking.